Person on Edge

MY thoughts, MY feelings, MY experiences

By Suzanne Drew

Contents

Devil by my side

Tick-tock tick-toc, the noise is getting louder, for the time is coming, the dreaded judgement hour.

There's a faint voice in the distance telling me to please just try, but the Devil on my shoulder, is telling me I'm not worthy of this life.

You see, I feel like I've failed, I've not lived up to be the person who everyone wanted me to be, but I did really try, it just clearly wasn't meant to be.

I don't want to wake up and keep feeling this pain every day, I just want it to stop, I just want it to go away.

So, I unscrew the cap and I count them one by one, knowing that if I proceed, my actions can never be undone.

Am I scared? Not one bit, I want this life to be over, I'm out, I quit.

<u>Why?</u>

The shivers, the nightmares and yes sometimes I cry, there'll always be times I ask myself why?

For what did I do to deserve so much trauma and pain? The fears from that moment play over and over in my brain.

I don't let people in, I build barriers and walls, but that's my way of coping, its not 'one size fits all'.

But I know its not just me and that there's others out there too, I can relate I know what you've been through.

But I'll fight through my demons and I won't let them drag me down, because I'll beat this in the end and I'll be the one standing proud.

Haunted by a keyboard

You don't know me or what I've been through, but you feel the need to leave hurtful comments, you really have no clue.

Why would you do this? I've never done anything to you, you've singled me out, what? for something to do?

The things your typing one day you might regret, after all I am a human being, I have feelings, or did you forget?

The cruel words that your using can have a knock-on effect and people deal with negative comments in way you wouldn't expect.

You think your clever, you might see it as a bit of fun, but the words that you type can never mentally be undone.

Cats got your tongue

I'm lost and I'm broken these words are unspoken, I scream and I shout but the words just won't come out.

I want to tell I really do, but they won't understand what I'm going through.

They'll tell me I'm fine and to just give it some time, they'll tell me these moments wont last and that in time they'll pass.

But they don't understand that these feeling haunt me every day, maybe they'll think I'm crazy and look at me in a certain way.

People might distance themselves, but I just need some help, I can't take the risk, so until then, I'll just keep it to myself.

Take me away

Key after key, line after line, I slowly begin to forget,
the previous moments in time.

The pain inside, it begins to pass, but I know it's
only temporary, I know it won't last.

My minds switched off, reality no longer exists, the
feeling of not feeling, this is something I've missed.

I can take on the world, I can be who I want to be,
nothing or no one is going to stand in the way, of
me being me.

I'm now in a world where all your troubles slip away,
oh what I'd give to have a magic button, a button
that says, 'press to replay'.

Torn

One minute I'm happy, the next I'm sad, one minute I'm reminiscing about the good times, the next I'm focussing on the bad.

Am I coming or am I going? What the hell is wrong with me? I wish I had a way of knowing.

I woke up happy, I got out on the right side of the bed, but now I'm on a downer, wishing I was dead.

One step forward, two steps back, my moods constantly changing, I can't stay on track.

I wish I was normal; I wish I could be like the others instead, but the reality is, I'm just a person, a person on edge.

I see you

They're always watching me, sometimes they follow me home, oh how I wish, I wish they'd just leave me alone.

I don't know what they want, why can't they just leave me be, they must think I'm blind when they hide, but trust me I can see.

Walking down the street, I hear the footsteps behind, I beg "please don't take me", I state it's not my time.

I pluck up the courage and I turn myself around, but to my surprise, I see nothing, nothing but the ground.

Where did they go? Maybe they went back to hide? Maybe something scared them off, or maybe I was just lucky this time.

Breathing Easy

It hurts so bad, the pain I feel inside, so I promise myself, I'll do it, just this one last time.

But I've made these promises to myself before, and I know I'll do it again, if not, several times more.

Rolling up my sleeve, I pick up the knife, I'm doing this to release the pain, not to end my life.

I keep it a secret because I know people won't understand, but it's my way of coping, I have the upper hand.

Because the feeling of cutting myself seems to let it all out, and for that moment in time, I can breathe again, and my troubles are forgotten about.

Meal after meal

I'm tired and its late, so I finish my meal and put my
knife and fork on my plate.

But suddenly I get this overwhelming urge, I run to
the bathroom and I make myself purge.

I return from the bathroom and I tell a little white
lie, I say there must have been something in the
food, that didn't agree with me this time.

I know its not right, but what am I supposed to
do? I can't have the best of both worlds, eat and
be skinny too.

So, I'll do the same for breakfast, lunch and dinner,
and I'll continue to do so, until I get thinner.

Hidden Truth

The nights going great, you forget all your troubles, you live for the moment, in your own little bubble.

But you check your watch so you can keep track of time, a curfew has been set and you dare not cross the line.

Because what scares you the most, is what awaits you at home, will this time be mild or will it result in broken bones.

Now the nights come to an end and you say goodbye to your friends, praying to yourself that you'll get to see them again.

You put your key in the door and you try to sneak in, the last thing you want to do, is disturb the monster that awaits within.

But the door is now locked, and there's things you wouldn't believe, for its behind closed doors, that the truth cannot be seen.

Mirror Mirror

You see them standing there, the look they give you,
with that judgemental glare.

They know what your thinking and what your all
about, from every insecurity to every little doubt.

From the shape of your body, to your nails
and your hair, why do they judge you? Why do
they even care?

But maybe in that moment they might give you
some slack, to pull yourself together and get
yourself back.

Because the pain you feel, they feel it to, because that
person you see, that person is you.

In a Pandemic

You want to go out, but you have to stay inside, you need to get out because its affecting your state of mind.

Deep within you break in time, but your scared to speak out just in case it dents your pride.

Its hard to adjust, but you know it's a must, these times are testing, but in faith you trust.

Its going to be tough, you'll be tested and tried, believe me I know, there's been many a nights, I've just laid there and cried.

I know your scared of losing yourself and who you are, but the real you is there and not so far.

De ja vu

So, you thought the bad times had gone away, but it's starting to look like that they may be here to stay.

You start to remember how much you overcame, and you're now starting to panic that you may have to live those days again.

Reflecting on the times where the darkness overshadowed the light, remembering the times when you thought the end was never in sight.

The uncertainty, the fear, its all creeping back, questioning how you'll manage this again, without going off track.

But remember you've done it before, so you can do it again, it's going to be hard, but please don't give in.

Catch me when I fall

If I was to sit here and tell you how I really feel, I think you'd be shocked and question whether these words were real.

I feel forgotten and lost, like I don't exist, do people remember me, am I actually being missed?

Because I've always been that person that's always had everyone's backs, maybe they think I don't need the support, maybe they think I'm stronger than that.

And I know these times are hard and everyone is feeling it too, but a lot of us keep it hidden, that's just what we do.

But its ok to let it out and have a little cry, each day is a test, all that matters is that we try.

Destiny

Its been three hours now, of walking in the rain, pondering my thoughts of how I get rid of this pain.

Step by step, I go over the options in my brain, from jumping off a bridge, to throwing myself in front of a train.

Maybe this is what they want, maybe I want it too? My heads so scrambled right now, I really don't have a clue.

I opt for the bridge and I slowly move near, my heart starts pounding and my head fills with fear.

But all of a sudden, I freeze in my tracks, I can't let go, somethings holding me back.

Maybe it's the thought of what I'll leave behind, or maybe it's just the fact, that it wasn't my time.

Uninvited

Laid in the dark, you can't get out of bed, anxiety and depression, they say its all in your head.

You don't want to go out because your scared of what might be, putting yourself out there, for all the world to see.

You have your dark moments and you can't explain why, you just have this overwhelming feeling, a feeling of wanting to die.

They say its easy to get out of, all you need to do is just try, but they don't understand that you have days, where all you do is cry.

You thought you had it all, you thought your life was good, how could something like this happen? you never thought it could.

See you thought you were in control, you thought you were in charge, but that's mental health for you, it catches you off guard.

In plain sight

I've spent many a times wishing I was a perfect ten, depriving my body and questioning when?

Why don't I look like them? oh how I wish that was me, the attention they get, its plain for everyone to see.

But what is it that I cannot see? maybe it's the media, maybe I'm blinded by me.

Because the way you look is not who you are, and if you think it is, you couldn't be further afar.

For we are all unique, not one person the same, its who you are inside, which makes you beautiful every day.

The clock doesn't stop

Maybe if I'd done this, or maybe if I'd done
that, it's what you keep thinking, but its what's
holding you back.

You need to stop torturing yourself with the ifs and
the whys, maybe things were meant to be, maybe it
was a blessing in disguise?

You see the paths that you take and the choices you
make, you think that's what controls your future,
some of us call it fate.

But destiny has a plan, it was decided from the
start, from the minute you entered this world, to the
minute you depart.

So, don't sit and question all the things that you've
done, because time waits for no one, and its
time to move on.

Hold on

These times are testing, its plain for everyone to see, but please tell yourself, its not the time to give up on being me.

Even though your struggling and its difficult to see, soon these days will be over, and soon you will be free.

Free to be the person you used to be, the person that was full of life, and so much positivity.

Just because some days are dark, it doesn't mean that the light cant still shine, through all the obstacles and barriers, tell yourself 'this life is mine'.

Its yours for the taking, so please don't give up, life's sent to test you, so remember that, and keep your chin up.

<u>Think about it</u>

You want what they have, why can't that be you, but through jealousy and spite, you may not have thought it through.

Because what you see and what is actually true, can be so far apart, compared to your point of view.

Because the pictures we paint can hide the truth we're in, nobody knows what a person is going through, or the struggles within.

You don't know about the loans they took out to get them cars, the eating disorders or the domestic abuse that left scars.

So now you know what you see is not always that clear, people keep things secret, through failure and fear.

So be thankful for what you've got, and please just be kind, because the grass isn't always greener, on the other side.

Blinded

Trapped in my thoughts, buried not so deep in my mind, I need to reach out, the pain, it makes me feel sick inside.

Should I speak out? Or is it too late? Surely people are out there, who've felt the same and can relate.

But where do I start? What do I do? maybe I need a sign, something to give me a clue.

Its so dark right now and I can't see the light, but by speaking out and getting some guidance, it might make me feel better, and maybe I'll regain my sight.

Because the truth is, there are people who care, we just need to pause for a second and know that help is there.

Thank you for taking the time to read my book.

Every poem that you have just read details some of the struggles I've gone through with regards to my Mental Health, some of which are still battles I fight on a daily basis.

I want you to know that you are not alone, and that there is help out there.

Take care and be kind to yourself x

Rethink Mental Illness

www.rethink.org

Samaritans

Call: 116 123

Crisis Text Line

Text SHOUT to 85258

CALM (for Men)

Call: 0800 58 58 58

Printed in Great Britain
by Amazon